North Riverside Public Library District
2400 S. Des Plaines Avenue
North Riverside, IL 60546
708-447-0869
www.northriversidelibrary.org

FOXES

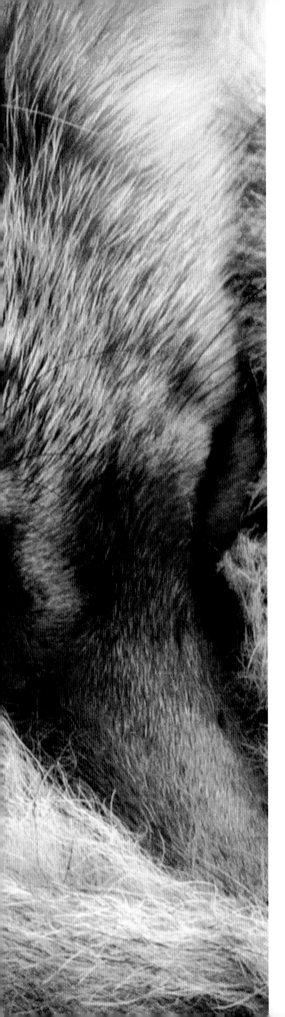

LIVING WILD

Published by Creative Education and Creative Paperbacks
P.O. Box 227, Mankato, Minnesota 56002
Creative Education and Creative Paperbacks are imprints of The Creative Company
www.thecreativecompany.us

Design and production by Mary Herrmann
Art direction by Rita Marshall
Printed in China

Photographs by Alamy (Moviestore collection Ltd), Creative Commons Wikimedia (Algkalv, Eyal Bartov, Bernd Blumhardt, Paul Bransom, Bernard DUPONT, g'pa bill, HelmutBoehm, Alfred Hutter, J. G. Keulemans, Utagawa Kuniyoshi, Sumeet Moghe, Tim Parkinson, Peterson B Moose, Profberger, Frans Snyders), Dreamstime (Brian Kushner), Getty Images (Feng Wei Photography), iStockphoto (bebecom98, DoxaDigital, GP232, Northof60), Project Gutenberg, Shutterstock (Max Allen, andamanec, dean bertoncelj, bukentagen, EcoPrint, Jorg Hackemann, Jamie Hall, Incredible Arctic, Matthew Jacques, Tory Kallman, l i g h t p o e t, Maksimilian, Stephan Morris, olga_gl, outdoorsman, Menno Schaefer, Betty Shelton, Andrew Swinbank, Sergey Timofeev, Arthur van der Kooij, Ivonne Wierink, yod67), Stephanie "Ace" Medlock

Library of Congress Cataloging-in-Publication Data
Gish, Melissa.
Foxes / Melissa Gish.
p. cm. — (Living wild)
Includes bibliographical references and index.
Summary: A look at foxes, including their habitats, physical characteristics such as their incredibly sensitive whiskers, behaviors, relationships with humans, and their often-misperceived status as a nuisance in the world today.

ISBN 978-1-60818-704-1 (hardcover)
ISBN 978-1-62832-300-9 (pbk)
ISBN 978-1-56660-740-7 (eBook)
1. Foxes—Juvenile literature. I. Title.

QL737.C22 G577 2016
599.775—dc23   2015026822

CCSS: RI.5.1, 2, 3, 8; RST.6-8.1, 2, 5, 6, 8; RH.6-8.3, 4, 5, 6, 7, 8

First Edition HC 9 8 7 6 5 4 3 2 1
First Edition PBK 9 8 7 6 5 4 3 2 1

CREATIVE EDUCATION • CREATIVE PAPERBACKS

FOXES

Melissa Gish

It is just before sunrise on India's Karakoram-West Tibetan Plateau.

A corsac fox silently descends a grassy slope.

It is just before sunrise on India's Karakoram–West Tibetan Plateau. A corsac fox silently descends a grassy slope. At more than 4,000 feet (1,219 m) above sea level, the treeless, frozen tundra is spattered with rocks and patches of snow. The fox spots a vole emerging from its nest. The vole's winter store of food is nearly exhausted. The small rodent wastes no time in dashing toward a nearby stream, unaware of the fox watching its every move. Despite coloration that masks the vole among the dry grass, the creature cannot escape the fox's gaze. The fox follows the vole undetected. At the edge of the stream, the vole stuffs its mouth with fresh, new grass. Suddenly, the fox leaps from behind a rock, pouncing on the vole with a crushing blow. As the sun rises over the Himalayas, the fox dines on its first meal of the day.

WHERE IN THE WORLD THEY LIVE

■ Red Fox
Northern
Hemisphere

■ Fennec Fox
Sahara Desert

■ Rüppell's Fox
North Africa,
Middle East,
southwestern Asia

■ Cape Fox
South Africa,
Botswana,
Zimbabwe

■ Arctic Fox
Arctic regions

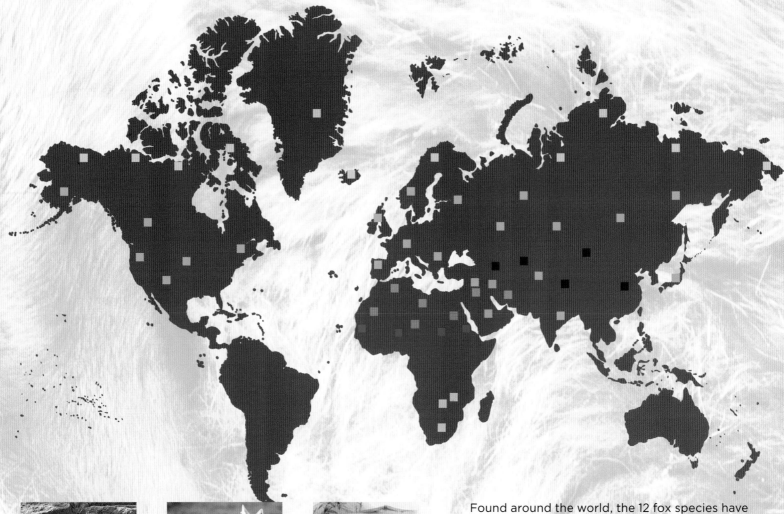

■ Blanford's Fox
Middle East

■ Corsac Fox
central Asia

■ Pale Fox
African Sahel
region

Found around the world, the 12 fox species have adapted to bitterly cold climates and searingly hot regions. Some species, such as the Arctic fox, thrive amidst the coldest habitats on Earth. Others, such as Rüppell's and fennec foxes, have adapted to survive in dry deserts. The colored squares represent areas in which eight fox species are found today.

FABULOUS FOXES

Foxes are found on every continent except Antarctica. They belong to the family Canidae, which includes domestic and wild dogs, wolves, jackals, coyotes, foxes, and several foxlike **mammals**. Foxes are smaller in size and have a flatter skull than their relatives. Though some fox relatives bear the name "fox" (including the gray and island foxes and the bat-eared fox), only members of the genus *Vulpes* are true foxes. All 12 species of true foxes are descended directly from a single ancestor. The term for such a group of animals is "clade," from a Greek word meaning "branch." Among all members of the dog family, true foxes make up one single group. Most foxes are carnivores, meaning they eat primarily meat. Red foxes have **adapted** to an omnivorous diet, meaning they eat both meat and plant matter. Such flexibility has allowed red foxes to thrive in both urban and rural habitats.

Foxes live in a variety of habitats around the world. While most species never encounter each other, a few species can **interbreed**. Fennec foxes are found only in North Africa, sharing habitat with Rüppell's foxes, which

Coyotes, members of the genus Canis, *are larger and more social than most of their fox cousins.*

Tibetan sand foxes are not an endangered species, for roughly 37,000 are estimated to exist in Tibet alone.

The Blanford's fox has sharp, curved claws and bare footpads useful for gripping narrow cliff ledges in its rocky habitat.

also occupy parts of the Middle East. Pale foxes live in a north-central region called the African Sahel, and Cape foxes inhabit only southern Africa. Blanford's foxes are spread from Egypt eastward to Afghanistan. In Asia, corsac foxes inhabit central regions, and Bengal foxes exist in India and surrounding countries. Tibetan sand foxes call the plateaus of western China, Tibet, Nepal, and neighboring countries home. A more widely distributed species is the Arctic fox, which is named for its frigid habitat of Earth's northernmost regions, from Alaska and Canada to Greenland, Iceland, Scandinavia, and Russia. In North America, the kit fox makes its home in Mexico and the western United States, while the swift fox lives in the grasslands of the Midwest. The red fox has the widest distribution of any fox, inhabiting most of the Northern Hemisphere. Nonnative red foxes also exist in Australia, where British colonists introduced them in 1845.

Male foxes, called dogs or tods, are typically 15 to 20 percent larger than females, called vixens. The largest fox species is the red fox, which varies in size depending on geographical location and availability of food. Red foxes in cold northern climates tend to be much bigger than foxes

In winter, a red fox's coat is twice as dense as it is in summer.

The corsac fox's name comes from the Russian word korsák, which refers to the animal's bushy tail.

in warmer climates. Red fox tods in the north stand about 16 inches (40.6 cm) tall at the shoulder. They can grow to nearly 3 feet (0.9 m) long—with an extra 12 inches (30.5 cm) of tail—and weigh as much as 30 pounds (13.6 kg). The average size of most red foxes, however, is about 15 pounds (6.8 kg). The fennec fox is the smallest of the dog family. About the height of a typical house cat, a fennec fox usually weighs no more than 3.5 pounds (1.6 kg). Its tail can be nearly as long as its body, and its ears half as long.

All fox species have long bodies with slender legs. Like other dogs, foxes have thick pads on the bottoms of their feet and walk on their toes. The four toes on each foot have claws used for holding down captured prey. The fox's dewclaw, located on the ankle of each front foot, is a remnant of prehistoric times and serves no purpose today. Foxes' bones are less dense than the bones of their relatives, making foxes lighter and swifter than other dogs of similar size. Red foxes easily trot at a speed of roughly eight miles (12.9 km) per hour. Their top running speed is 30 miles (48.3 km) per hour—faster than a human.

Other distinguishing characteristics of the fox include its long, bushy tail; sharply pointed, upright ears; and

With its powerful legs, the fennec fox can jump straight up in the air two feet (0.6 m), or three times its own height.

Foxes' narrow snouts allow them to snatch prey hiding in small spaces.

Tibetan sand foxes are not nocturnal because their main prey (pikas, marmots, and lizards) are active during the day.

long, slender snout. The fox's nose is surrounded by dozens of soft, black whiskers that are much longer than other dogs'. These whiskers, called vibrissae, are attached to sensitive nerve cells beneath the skin of the fox's face. The fox has similar (but shorter) vibrissae on the front of its forelegs. As a fox moves past objects, it can detect other motion through vibrations—even under snow. A fox can also feel air currents with its whiskers, which may alert it to approaching danger. As a skilled hunter, the fox is equipped with a keen sense of hearing. A fox can identify the positions of earthworms underground and mice beneath three feet (0.9 m) of snow. Despite having 42 teeth, the fox does not chew its food. Using its 13 pairs of grinding teeth along the sides of the jaws, a fox simply crushes and swallows small prey such as grasshoppers, shrews, and baby birds. Two pairs of sharp upper and lower canine teeth and six pairs of pointed incisors at the front of the mouth slice larger prey into small pieces.

Foxes are more active at night than during the day, so they are able to see well in low light. Movement also catches their attention. Their eyes contain a reflective layer

When fighting over the best feeding grounds, the strongest fox usually wins rights to the territory.

The Arctic fox's dark eyes function like sunglasses, protecting the fox's eyes from snow glare.

of tissue called a tapetum lucidum. This tissue collects light and concentrates it at the center of the **retina**. The tissue also causes eyeshine, making the eyes reflect color when a light is shined on them. Fox eyeshine varies from yellow to green. Because foxes are more sensitive to light, their **pupils** are different from other dogs'. When the fox's pupil shrinks to let in less light, it becomes a vertical slit (like that of a cat's eye). This prevents too much light from entering the eye and causing damage.

A fox's furry coat is called pelage. Arctic foxes have two layers of fur to keep them warm: dense underfur and long, hollow guard hairs that trap warm air to provide the fox with **insulation** from the winter's cold. From December through February, that pelage is white and very thick. It starts to thin out from March through June and changes to a browner color. Other cold-climate fox species also shed their winter coats in summer, but foxes that live in consistently warm climates have shorter, thinner coats year round. Desert foxes also have larger ears than their kin. Big ears help to release heat from the foxes' bodies. In addition, foxes sweat from the pads of their feet and pant to cool down.

Humans have about 400 scent receptors in their noses, but foxes have more than 200 million.

The common term for a group of foxes is a "skulk," a word that relates to their stealthy movements.

WHAT DOES THE FOX SAY?

Some foxes' multicolored coats help them hide from predators.

Foxes kept safely in zoos or as pets can live as long as 10 to 14 years. However, foxes usually survive only three to five years in the wild. There they face predators such as bears, wolves, big cats, hyenas, and eagles, as well as diseases such as rabies, mange, and canine distemper. The changing global climate affects their ability to find suitable food and shelter. But humans pose the greatest threat to foxes. People trap and hunt the animals and disrupt or destroy their natural habitats. Foxes are not fussy eaters but are instead opportunistic feeders, meaning they will eat any kind of prey they can catch, from worms and beetles to mice, birds, and rabbits. They will also eat eggs and berries if available. This flexible diet makes foxes highly adaptable animals, able to survive in remote environments as well as urban areas.

Most fox species share a particular area called a home range among 3 to 15 individuals. (The **solitary** red fox is an exception.) Foxes are mostly active at night and typically hunt alone. During fair weather, they sleep outdoors under bushes or in hollow logs. During harsher conditions, they

Rüppell's and fennec foxes have fur covering their footpads to protect their feet from the scorching desert sand.

Young foxes learn everything they need to know about survival from their mothers and older female siblings.

sleep in burrows dug into soft soil, usually in hillsides or at the base of trees or shrubs. A room at the end of the burrow is called a den. Foxes sometimes use dens abandoned by other animals, such as badgers and wolves.

A fox has numerous dens within its home range. The size of a home range varies according to geographical location as well as the availability of food and mates. Foxes that live in urban areas may inhabit less than eight square city blocks of territory, while rural foxes may have home ranges exceeding seven square miles (18.1 sq km). Because of the scarcity of food, Arctic fox home ranges average 13 square miles (33.7 sq km). In remote desert climates, the home ranges of African and Asian foxes may be as large as 20 square miles (51.8 sq km). Male and female red foxes' home ranges tend to overlap, but male red foxes share space only in areas where food is plentiful. Where resources are scarce, red foxes defend their territory by chasing away intruders or, if necessary, fighting with rivals.

A fox patrols the boundaries of its territory, leaving various signs that alert other foxes to its presence in the area. It drops **feces** or sprays urine on the home range's borders. Sometimes a fox sprays its droppings with a bacteria-rich fluid produced by special **glands** near the anal region. The fox regularly marks particular landmarks such as fence posts, stumps, and rocks with urine so that the scent remains fresh at all times. This behavior, called scent marking, is one of the principal means of fox communication.

Foxes also communicate with each other by using more vocalizations than any other dog. The alarm call, used to signal danger, is short and quick as if the fox is saying "Ow!" Mother foxes use the call to chase their offspring into a hiding place. Gekkering is a chattering sound similar to birds trilling or chickens clucking. Foxes utter this

Unlike other foxes, corsac foxes do not defend home ranges and may form hunting packs in winter.

Arctic foxes sporting their darker summer pelage are sometimes called blue foxes.

sound while playing or fighting. A fox uses the bark-and-scream to let other foxes know of its presence. It sounds like "woo-woo-woo-woo-wah," with the final note drawn out like a scream. Among other fox sounds that send messages across home ranges are short, high-pitched cries and long, whistling howls. A shrill "wah" sound called the vixen's scream is uttered back and forth between males and females, particularly during mating season.

In late fall, foxes begin traveling through their overlapping home ranges in search of mates. They use scent marking and vocalization to indicate their availability. Once two foxes select each other, the pair will spend several weeks getting acquainted. Although they continue to hunt alone, they stay in contact by vocalizing. After hunting, mates play together, chasing each other and rolling around on the ground. They also sleep in the same den. Some fox species, such as kit foxes, mate for life, but other mating pairs reconnect only when other potential mates are unavailable. By winter, the fox pair is ready to reproduce. Vixens can become pregnant for a period of only about three days per season. In warm climates, this occurs in December,

Mouthing is a behavior that fox relatives or mating pairs often exhibit when greeting one another.

Kit foxes may sometimes be mistaken for desert gray foxes, but kit foxes have much larger ears.

but farther north, vixens may not be ready to breed until as late as March.

The average **gestation** period for foxes is 52 days. Shortly before she gives birth, the female selects a birthing den, and the male is not allowed to share it. Up to 12 kits are born, with 4 to 6 being most common. Newborn red fox kits weigh about four ounces (113 g), while fennec fox kits are less than half this size. The kits are born blind and deaf, and they are covered with dark brown fur. The mother fox stays with her kits for the first two weeks of their lives—until their eyes and ears open—relying on her mate to bring her food. The mother fox feeds her offspring milk, but when they are four weeks old, she begins to supplement their diet with solid food that she **regurgitates**. The kits follow their mother out of the den and begin to mimic her hunting behavior, pouncing on insects and leaves. Female offspring from the previous year whose home ranges overlap with their mother's may return to help care for their new siblings. Known as helper vixens, these females clean and groom the kits, play with them, bring them food, and teach them survival tactics.

The kits are **weaned** by about eight weeks old. Within another month, their pelage begins to change to its adult coloration. They accompany their parents on hunting trips away from the den, learning valuable skills. The father fox eventually returns to his own home range, and by the time the young foxes are six months old, they, too, leave the mother fox. Females may stay close by, but males are generally chased away from their parents' home ranges. Once the young foxes establish their own home ranges and are about 10 months old, they begin scent marking and vocalizing to attract mates—thus beginning the fox life cycle all over again.

A close relative of true foxes, bat-eared foxes survive on a diet of mostly insects on the African plains.

While hunting for kangaroo rats and black-tailed jackrabbits, kit foxes may travel up to two miles (3.2 km) each night.

The nine-tailed fox was a popular subject in the 400-year-old Japanese art form called Ukiyo-e.

In its southernmost habitat, the Arctic fox's coat may feature both light and dark coloration year round.

ew animals have a longer or more diverse **cultural** history than foxes. These animals appear in the legends and **mythology** of most civilizations on Earth. Many stories depict the fox's beauty and intelligence, but just as many represent foxes as cunning tricksters that should not be trusted. Some cultures view foxes as creatures with great power. In Finland, the aurora borealis, or northern lights, are called *revontulet*, meaning "foxfire." A legend from the Sami people (who are **indigenous** to parts of far northern Sweden, Norway, Finland, and Russia) tells how the fox runs over the hills and mountains, dashing its tail into the snow and sending sparks of light into the sky.

The Arctic fox's ability to change the color of its coat gave rise to a legend that varies among the indigenous peoples of the Arctic, including the Koryak of Russia and the Inuit of Greenland, Canada, and the U.S. To escape the cold, the story goes, a fox sneaked into a man's home and removed its fur so that it magically took on the appearance of a woman. The man came to adore the woman and married her. However, as the winter wore

Arctic foxes do not shiver until the temperature falls to -94 °F (-70 °C)—almost as cold as Siberia's record low!

on, the fox-woman began to smell bad—as wild foxes tend to do. The man complained, which hurt his wife's feelings. She put her fur back on and ran away, living to this day all alone on the frozen landscape.

Historically, foxes were sometimes viewed as trustworthy, honorable, and even sacred animals. A fox served as the messenger for the goddess Ninhursag in stories of Mesopotamia from 4000 B.C. In Japanese folklore, white foxes were the messengers of Inari Okami, the spirit of agriculture. Stories about *kitsune* (the Japanese word for "fox") describe magical foxes that can grant wishes, play tricks on people, and even transform into humans. From the 14th through 16th centuries, Japanese storytellers contributed to a collection of about 350 tales called the *Otogizoshi*. Among the stories are those of a nine-tailed fox, who is not only cunning and dangerous to humans but also nearly indestructible. In Chinese stories, the nine-tailed fox's spirit can possess humans and make them follow its commands. And in Korean tales, the nine-tailed fox devours people in order to live longer. The Asian myths of nine-tailed foxes have lived on as the Pokémon character Ninetales, the video game *League of*

Legends' character Ahri, and the manga series *Omamori Himari*'s primary villain, Tamamo-no-mae.

Foxes are also portrayed as tricksters. In a fable from Aesop, the legendary Greek storyteller, a fox plays a mean trick on a stork. He serves delicious fish soup in a wide, shallow bowl and laughs as the stork can do nothing more than dip the tip of his long bill into the bowl. A tale from

Flemish artist Frans Snyder's 17th-century illustration shows how, in Aesop's fable, the stork repays the fox for his trickery by serving dinner in a tall, thin jar that the fox cannot reach.

THE·CAT·AND·THE·FOX.

The cat and fox, each like a little saint,
On pious pilgrimage together went;
Two real Tartufes, two Patelins, birds of prey,
Soft-footed rogues, who paid or cleared the way,
Picking the bones of poultry, stealing cheese,
Rivalling each other. They the road to ease,
For it was tedious and long,
Oft shortened by contentions sharp and strong.
Dispute's a very happy source;
Without it restless souls would sleep of course.
Our pilgrims with it made each other hoarse,
Quarreled their fill, then dirt on neighbors cast.
Reynard said to the cat at last:
"Pretender, are you better skilled than I,
Who could with tricks a hundred cats supply?"
"No," said the cat, "I only boast of one,
But that's worth any thousand known."
Ready again their quarrel to begin,
With "Yes" and "No," through thick and thin,

The pack alarmed them, silencing their din.
"Friend," cried the cat, "now search your cunning brain,
Examine all your tricks, and search again
For some sure plan — mine's ready, do you see?"
He said, and quick sprang up a lofty tree.
Sly Reynard played a hundred pranks in vain,
Entered a hundred holes — escaped assault,
Put Finder and his brothers in default;
He sought asylum all around,
But he nowhere asylum found.
They watched the burrow where he hid so sly,
And smoked him out — two terriers were nigh,
Who worried him as he went bounding by.
Avoid too many schemes; there ruin lies;
For while we choose, the happy moment flies.
Have but one plan, and let that plan be wise.

from The Fables of La Fontaine,
by Jean de La Fontaine (1621–95)

the Menominee Indians of Wisconsin tells how the fox tricked the wolf out of a basket of maple sugar. The fox convinced the wolf to cut a hole in the ice of a frozen pond and use his tail as a lure to catch fish for eating with the maple sugar. But the hole froze shut, trapping the wolf and leaving all the maple sugar for the fox.

In some stories, foxes boast of their cleverness but find they are not as smart as their fellow animals. A folk tale from Romania tells of a fox and a hedgehog that fell into a hole dug by a farmer who was tired of the fox raiding his chicken yard. The hedgehog complained of feeling sick, so the fox took the hedgehog in his mouth and threw him out of the hole. But the fox had no idea how to get out himself. The hedgehog told the fox to play dead and lie stiff as a board. Then the farmer, thinking the fox dead, threw him out of the hole, allowing the animal to escape into the woods. A myth from the Delaware Indians of the northeastern U.S. explains why the fox's mouth and lips are black. One day, the sun came too close to Earth and began to bake the land. The fox volunteered to carry the sun back to the sky, but when he took the sun in his mouth, it burned him.

A 1921 collection of fables retold the Menominee Indian tale using a bear instead of the wolf.

Foxes in classic literature reflect traditional characteristics of cunning and trickery as well. The sneaky fox Mr. Tod first appeared in Beatrix Potter's book *The Tale of Jemima Puddle-Duck* in 1908. He got his own book, *The Tale of Mr. Tod*, in 1912. Reddy Fox, a clever fox character created by American author and conservationist Thornton Burgess, first appeared in the 1913 book *The Adventures of Reddy Fox*. Foxes continue to entertain in modern literature and film. Brian Jacques's Redwall series (1986–2011) features a number of foxes: the **apothecary** Fortunata, a warrior named Urgan Nagru, and the vengeful ship captain Vizka Longtooth. Perhaps the best-known literary fox is the nameless character that appears in the Dr. Seuss tongue-twister *Fox in Socks* (1965). Beloved film foxes include Robin Hood, star of the 1973 Walt Disney animated feature, and the family featured in *Fantastic Mr. Fox*, the 2009 stop-motion animated film based on Roald Dahl's 1970 novel.

The 1967 book *The Fox and the Hound* by Daniel P. Mannix features two mortal enemies: a fox named Tod and a hunting dog named Copper. In 1981, Walt Disney's animated version of the story turned the pair into friends.

In 2006, *The Fox and the Hound 2* was released directly to video. The latter film takes place during Tod and Copper's teen years. The pair's relationship is complicated because of the long history of violence associated with foxes and hunting dogs. Originating in Great Britain in the 16th century, the sport of fox hunting involved foxes being chased by packs of dogs, or hounds, trained to follow the foxes' scent. Once the hounds cornered a fox, the hunter would shoot it. The practice was banned in Britain in 2005 but continues in many countries, including Canada, the U.S., and Australia, where foxes were imported specifically for fox hunting in 1845.

The Fox and the Hound *was Walt Disney's first animated feature to use computer graphics.*

*One of the earliest fox ancestors,
Carnivora miacidae was smaller
than most of today's foxes.*

SHARING THE WORLD WITH FOXES

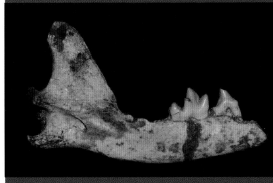

A lower jawbone with teeth is the only known evidence of the fox ancestor Vulpes skinneri.

The earliest ancestors of foxes were a group of catlike mammals called miacids that emerged about 60 million years ago. As miacids evolved, or changed, some (including mongooses and civets) remained tree-dwelling and catlike, while others became doglike. The first true canid evolved about 40 million years ago. Named *Prohesperocyon wilsoni* in 1994, its fossil remains were found in what is now southwestern Texas. It resembled a raccoon dog, which is a fox cousin native to Asia. Canids continued to evolve into different groups, each specifically suited to the varying environments throughout which they spread.

In 2013, Dr. Brian Kuhn of Wits University's Institute for Human Evolution, located in Johannesburg, South Africa, and a team of fellow scientists discovered the fossils of a previously unknown fox ancestor, which they named *Vulpes skinneri*. The fossils of a lower jawbone and teeth are those of a fox that existed about 2 million years ago—roughly the same time that the first humans evolved. Fox fossils have rarely been found in Africa, and the team's discovery may be able to offer new information

The desert-dwelling pale fox is able to get enough moisture from its food so that it rarely needs to drink water.

on the ways early humans and small mammals shared the region.

Older fox fossils were discovered in Tibet's Zanda Basin and Kunlun Mountains between 2006 and 2012. Scientists calculate that the 3 fossilized jaws with teeth are up to 5 million years old. Scientists believe that the prehistoric fox, *Vulpes qiuzhudingi*, was an Arctic fox ancestor because its teeth are extra sharp, similar to those of modern Arctic foxes. Unlike other foxes, which may eat plants, berries, and nuts in addition to meat, Arctic foxes are hypercarnivores, feeding almost exclusively on meat. The prehistoric fox was about 20 percent larger than today's Arctic fox—about the size of the red fox.

The smallest fox species is also the most endangered. The San Joaquin (*SAN wa-KEEN*) kit fox, a subspecies found only in scattered parts of California, has been officially listed as an endangered species by the U.S. Fish and Wildlife Service since 1967. Despite various recovery efforts as well as a ban on hunting and trapping, the San Joaquin kit fox's numbers continue to decline annually. Fewer than 7,000 of these foxes exist. The disappearance of gray wolves from California by the early 20th century

had led to a rise in the coyote population—and coyotes prey heavily on kit foxes. Today, the greatest threat to San Joaquin kit foxes is habitat loss, as humans continue to turn wilderness into urban and industrial areas. Currently, the California Rangeland Conservation Coalition is working to restore and protect 13 million acres (5.3 million ha) of the San Joaquin Valley for wildlife, including the endangered kit foxes.

Another fox species that receives legal protection is the swift fox, which is listed as endangered in Canada by the Committee on the Status of Endangered Wildlife in

San Joaquin kit foxes are fitted with lightweight radio collars as part of conservation efforts.

Conservationists are concerned that the Keystone Pipeline System could further disturb swift fox habitats.

Canada (COSEWIC). In the U.S., the swift fox is under consideration for endangered status, but more research is needed before an official determination can be made. In Colorado, New Mexico, and Wyoming, swift foxes are abundant. However, by the 1930s, overhunting had led to the swift fox's disappearance from its former range across the Great Plains from western Canada to Texas. Only scattered populations exist there today. In 1998, the Blackfeet Indians of northern Montana began a four-year program to raise and release **captive-reared** swift foxes. With the release of 123 foxes in 2002, a healthy population of swift foxes soon spread across northern Montana and southern Saskatchewan. To continue the effort to save swift foxes from **extinction**, the Assiniboine and Sioux Indians of eastern Montana began a similar reintroduction program in 2006.

Other fox species are in trouble as well. Southern Africa's Cape fox has been struggling to survive in a changing **ecosystem**. Dr. Jan F. Kamler, an American biologist in the Wildlife Conservation Research Unit at Oxford University, conducted a major study of Cape foxes from 2005 to 2008. Kamler discovered that the decline in Cape fox numbers coincided with the overhunting of leopards and other large predators in fox habitats. Without the threat of leopards, black-backed jackals thrived. More than twice the size of Cape foxes, these jackals preyed heavily on foxes. Kamler found that more than 70 percent of fox deaths could be attributed to black-backed jackals. Kamler explained, "By removing the large carnivores, especially leopards, we caused a chain reaction among all the remaining carnivores in the ecosystem."

Cape foxes sometimes hunt lambs, which causes farmers to view the foxes as a nuisance.

In its native India, the Bengal fox is routinely killed for use in tribal rituals and traditional medicine as well as for food.

A similar situation has had an opposite effect on the red fox. Its numbers have swelled in many areas around the world because of reduced hunting and lack of predators. Although healthy foxes shy away from people, they do not fear small farm animals, particularly poultry. Foxes are considered **nuisance** animals in Canada, the U.S., and other countries, and those caught raiding chicken pens or otherwise troubling farmers are often trapped, poisoned, and shot. Urban foxes, on the other hand, are often not only tolerated but also appreciated because their diet of mice and rats provides natural pest control. Since fox hunting was outlawed in Britain, the red fox population has exploded. There are an estimated 33,000 urban foxes in London alone. People often set out food for foxes, encouraging them to visit at night. Disturbing a wild animal's normal behavior can have unintended consequences, however, and cities such as London are now faced with too many foxes.

While foxes are not aggressive and pose no natural threat to humans, those that carry rabies may attack and bite people. Rabies is a disease affecting the brain that is fatal in animals and can be fatal in humans if left

untreated. Observing foxes from a distance can be safe and entertaining, but one should never approach a wild fox. There is a lot more to foxes than meets the eye. Research and education on the myriad foxes around the world are vital if we are to understand and appreciate the unique niche these fascinating creatures fill in our global ecosystem.

A fox that has discovered human trash will eagerly move into an urban area in search of easy meals.

ANIMAL TALE: HOW THE FOX OUTSMARTED A SEA MONSTER

Animal origins are part of traditional Jewish mythology. One of the most important and frightening creatures is the Leviathan, an enormous sea serpent so large and powerful that it was said to cause the ocean waves and create storms that churned the sea. In this Jewish myth, the fox plots to outsmart the Leviathan.

In the first days of creation, the oceans were empty except for the Leviathan, a monstrous creature so fierce that smoke poured from his nostrils and fire shot from his mouth. He was the king of the sea, but he had no subjects.

Then the Angel of Death was sent to fill the seas with life. He did this by drowning one member of each kind of land animal and transforming it into a sea creature. The Angel made lionfish, parrotfish, and catfish. He made tiger sharks, dogfish, and eagle rays. They all fell under the rule of the Leviathan.

The fox knew he was next. He sat down on a rock overlooking the ocean, pondering how he could escape a future as a fish. He looked down into the water and saw his reflection.

The Angel of Death came to the fox, who immediately began to cry. "No sense crying," the Angel said. "It's your turn."

"I'm not crying for myself," the fox said. "I'm crying because my friend wished to become a foxfish and threw himself into the sea before you arrived." The fox pointed to his reflection in the water. "Look!" he cried.

"Very good," said the Angel. Then he flew away.

Fox's plan worked for a year, but then the Leviathan counted his subjects. "Goosefish, honeycomb cowfish," he called out. "Sea robin, frogfish, fox—what's this?!" The Leviathan realized there was no foxfish.

Angry, the Leviathan created a terrible storm. "Why is there no foxfish?" he demanded. The shy porcupine fish told the Leviathan how the fox had tricked the Angel of Death. The Leviathan called to the catfish, "Bring me the fox. I will eat his heart. Tell him I am dying and have named him King of the Sea in my place."

The catfish went to the fox and gave him the Leviathan's message. Anxious to become a king, the fox jumped onto the catfish's back. As he carried the fox out to sea, the catfish began to laugh.

"What's so funny?" the fox asked.

Not one to keep a secret, the catfish told the fox the real reason the Leviathan wanted him.

"He's going to eat my heart?" the fox cried. "I wish you had told me that earlier. I do not carry my heart with me. I left it in my burrow. We must go back and get it."

The catfish did not want to take the fox to the Leviathan without his heart, so he turned back for shore. When they reached land, the fox instantly ran away, laughing at the catfish for being so foolish.

The catfish was afraid to return to the Leviathan and instead traveled up a river and hid beneath the bank. He has remained there to this day, afraid to face his ruler's wrath. And you will never see a fox by the seashore, for he stays far away from the eyes of the Leviathan.

GLOSSARY

adapted – changed to improve its chances of survival in its environment

apothecary – a historical name for someone who made and dispensed medicine

captive-reared – raised in a place from which escape is not possible

cultural – of or relating to particular groups in a society that share behaviors and characteristics that are accepted as normal by that group

ecosystem – a community of organisms that live together in an environment

extinction – the act or process of becoming extinct; coming to an end or dying out

feces – waste matter eliminated from the body

gestation – the period of time it takes a baby to develop inside its mother's womb

glands – organs in a human or animal body that produce chemical substances used by other parts of the body

indigenous – originating in a particular region or country

insulation – the state of being protected from the loss of heat

interbreed – reproduce through mating with a different species

mammals – warm-blooded animals that have a backbone and hair or fur, give birth to live young, and produce milk to feed their young

mythology – a collection of myths, or popular, traditional beliefs or stories that explain how something came to be or that are associated with a person or object

nuisance – something annoying or harmful to people or the land

pupils – the dark, circular openings in the center of the eyes through which light passes

regurgitates – throws up partially digested food

retina – a layer or lining in the back of the eye that is sensitive to light

solitary – alone, without companions

weaned – made the young of a mammal accept food other than nursing milk

SELECTED BIBLIOGRAPHY

Hunter, Luke. *Carnivores of the World*. Princeton, N.J.: Princeton University Press, 2011.

Kierepka, Elizabeth. Animal Diversity Web. "*Vulpes rueppellii*." http://animaldiversity.ummz.umich.edu/accounts /Vulpes_rueppellii.

Menino, Holly. *Darwin's Fox and My Coyote*. Charlottesville: University of Virginia Press, 2008.

National Geographic. "Red Fox." http://animals .nationalgeographic.com/animals/mammals/red-fox.

Rogers, Lesley J., and Gisela Kaplan. *Spirit of the Wild Dog: The World of Wolves, Coyotes, Foxes, Jackals and Dingoes*. New South Wales, Australia: Allen & Unwin, 2003.

Sovada, Marsha A., and Ludwig Carbyn, eds. *The Swift Fox: Ecology and Conservation of Swift Foxes in a Changing World*. Saskatchewan, Canada: University of Regina Press, 2003.

Note: Every effort has been made to ensure that any websites listed above were active at the time of publication. However, because of the nature of the Internet, it is impossible to guarantee that these sites will remain active indefinitely or that their contents will not be altered.

The fox's natural instinct to evade humans has made its survival more possible in a changing world.

INDEX